Buried By Baptism

by

W.B. Godbey

First Fruits Press
Wilmore,
Kentucky
c2018

Buried by Baptism.
By W.B. Godbey.
First Fruits Press, © 2018

ISBN: 978162718338 (print), 9781621718345 (digital), 9781621718352 (kindle)

Digital version at https://place.asburyseminary.edu/godbey/19/

Godbey, W. B. (William Baxter), 1833-1920.
    Buried by Baptism / by W.B. Godbey. – Wilmore, KY : First Fruits Press, ©2018.

    pages 36 ; cm.

    Reprint. Previously published: Greensboro, N.C. : Apostolic Messenger Office, [190-?]
    ISBN: 978162718338 (print)

    1. Baptism.   I. Title.

BV812.G622 2018

Cover design by Jon Ramsay

asburyseminary.edu
800.2ASBURY
204 North Lexington Avenue
Wilmore, Kentucky 40390

First Fruits
THE ACADEMIC OPEN PRESS OF ASBURY SEMINARY

First Fruits Press
The Academic Open Press of Asbury Theological Seminary
204 N. Lexington Ave., Wilmore, KY 40390
859-858-2236
first.fruits@asburyseminary.edu
asbury.to/firstfruits

Buried by Baptism

By

W. B. Godbey

AUTHOR OF
"New Testament Commentaries" "New Testament
Translation," and a great number of
other books and booklets.

PUBLISHED BY

APOSTOLIC MESSENGER OFFICE

900 SILVER RUN AVE.

GREENSBORO, N. C.

Buried by Baptism

The question naturally arises, "What is the thing buried?" The Bible is its own dictionary, leaving us without excuse. Lord give us the submissive humility of little Samuel whom Thou didst call to the prophetic office in his infancy and he meekly responded, "Speak Lord, for Thy servant heareth." We all came into this world ignorant as pigs and puppies; knowing nothing at all except Thou didst teach us. By this wonderful Word we are saved, sanctified, fed, panoplied, have the victory and will be judged in the great day. It is silly and foolish in us to study the Bible from a creedistical standpoint; as we are all hastening to the bar of God where we will be judged by the Bible alone. Therefore we should be dead to every clamor of human voice. Between us and the inspired Biblical authors, intervenes a period of eighteen hundred years, one thousand years of which is a black night with nothing but sacerdotalism, superstition, ignorance and priestcraft; during which the priest that could invent the most ceremonies, was considered the smartest. In view of this fact, this long dismal night intervening between us and the Apostolic Age, should be an ample admonition to us all to leap over the intervening chasm on the wings of triumphant faith, light down amid the effulgent blaze of pure and unadulterated inspired truth and shout the praises of God for His unutterable goodness, thus perfectly fortifying us against all the superstitious inovations of sacerdotalism and permitting us to stand face to face with our blessed heavenly Father on the sure foundation of His infallible Word and hear Him speak, as he did to Moses on Mt. Sinai, when He revealed His truth and Moses wrote it on tables of stone. Then let the battle cry ring around the world, "Back to the Bible.

Chapter I.

WHAT IS THE THING BURIED, INTO WHAT AND BY WHAT?

N. B. We have left the cavilings of Dark Age superstition, in which a thousand things were hatched and stuck like barnacles to the ship, and so many of them still clinging to the visible Church, enslaving the uncultured people as they are pertinaceously advocated by ignorant preachers and held up as genuine Gospel truth, when you search the Bible in vain to find a vestige of them, demonstrative truth, that they are post-apostolical in their origin, many of them having been brought in by the pagans, unheard of in the Bible.

(a) Romans 6: 5, 6 tells us about the burial and the sepulchre and the undertaker who buries the corpse. We do not bury the living, but the dead. The thing buried is not your mortal body. If it applied to it, death must precede the burial, which is not true; but all the people who teach the burial of the body as a fulfillment of these scriptures; all buried alive, irreconcilably contradictory of the truth and gross pandering to ignorance and superstition. The thing buried, as plainly revealed in God's Word, is not the mortal body at all, but the "old man," i. e., devil nature denominated "old" because it is as old as the devil, dating back to the fall of Lucifer, (Isa. 14: 12) : "How art thou fallen, O Lucifer, the son of the morning." This "old man," is not your mortal body, but the body of sin and not buried till after it is killed by crucifixion. If our Savior and apostles had lived in the Anglo-Saxon Age, they would all have been hung. But as they lived in the Roman Age, when they did not hang criminals but crucified them, they were all executed in that way. In this way Jesus, as our substitute, took our place and paid for us the death penalty. Our only chance to escape the death penalty—"The soul that sinneth it shall die"—is to follow Him to Gethsemane and in soul agony give up all of the world. Then follow Him to Calvary, suffer and die on the cross, be buried, not into water, but into "His death," which is the atonement He made for the sins of the whole world, and leaving the old crucified body of sin in that sepulchre forever, we "rise to walk in newness of life."

(b) The dogma that the physical body is the body of sin, is paganistic infidelity and superstition. It is the first heresy that got into the Church, even before the apostle John went to heaven. Consequently he exposes it in his epistles. Paul (2 Cor. 6:18) sweeps it from the field, "all sin is without the body," i. e., outside of it and not in it. He elucidates that fact, "he that committeth fornication, sins against his own body"; so does the drunkard. "For this reason the wicked shall not live out half of their days, because they shorten their life by dissipation." The immersion of the physical body in water is a gross conservation of this old paganistic infidelity, teaching that the body is the sinner; not a word of truth in it, and never was. Instead of my body being the sinner, it is the unfortunate victim of sin, suffering a thousand deaths by dissipation and debauchery, going down to a premature grave and into an awful eternity unprepared. Again the advocates of the immersion dogma, administer it with their own hands, whereas in this scripture it is buried by the baptism of the Holy Ghost, which also crucifies the "old man," and buries him in the death of Christ. These stupendous operations, crucifixion, destruction and interment, are all performed by the baptism which Jesus gives with the Holy

Ghost and fire.   Water is not mentioned in the entire book of Romans and Colossians in which we have
the record of the crucifixion, death and interment.

(c)   The humbugability of fallen humanity is
paradoxical in the extreme, and especially in religion, where Dr. Talmage says they do not take their
common sense, as they do in everything else.   The
baptism of the Holy Ghost is here personified as the
sheriff of the divine government, arresting the crim-
inal, and executing him, then going on and perform-
ing the office of undertaker, burying him in the atonement, into which every sin personality shall be buried or into hell.   It does not say that the baptism
is the burial, but the burier.   The imputation of all
these mighty works, crucifixion, destruction, burial
and resurrection to water baptism is not only flatly
contradictory of the plain Word, but a travesty on all
common sense, as you have nothing to do but use
the honest gumption which God has given you to see
clearly that there is not a drop of water in a million
miles of it, and no one will ever see it unless he has
water on the brain, hydrocephalus, which by the
medical world has been pronounced incurable.   That
is true, but Jesus can cure it, for I have tested and
proved Him.   I had it badly, in my youth, brought
up in the hotbed of Campbellism, blest in a Baptist
revival, and educated in a Baptist college.   Consequently when under conviction for sanctification and
no Holiness people to tell me how to get it; many
telling me, "Get immersed and you will be all right,
and have the victory."   Consequently I constrained a
Methodist to immerse me.   With deep reluctance, he
did me this service.   I took it in good faith sanguine-
ly, hoping that I would get the victory over all my
doubts and fears and the glorious liberty for which I
sighed, that I might, with a clean heart, filled with
perfect love, serve the Lord in the beauty of holiness.

All my sanguine anticipation evanesced when I found the change only from dry to wet, and that old Adam could live in the water as well as on dry land, amphibious, like the snake and the frog, his cousins. Then I wandered in the wilderness nineteen years, preaching fifteen of those years; as the Lord would not baptize me with the Holy Ghost and fire until I lost sight of the water god. I had no Holiness people to help me. Of course if I had been environed by bright witnesses to the Spirit, assisted by their prayers and testimonies I would have reached Beulad Land much sooner. I verily believe tinkering with the water god was Satan's potent enginery in keeping me in the wilderness so long. Finally in the midst of a glorious revival in which I was doing all the preaching; house full and altar crowded seeking regeneration as there were no witnesses to sanctification, I found myself in a large place; my gods having all retired to the dormitories; as having been born a Methodist, I had a group of little Methodist gods, and having become Baptistic on ordinances and graduated in a Baptist college, the water god was the biggest of all and the last to evanesce, disappearing in a fog bank, out of which he has never returned, thus finding myself in a large place. I saw none but Jesus. Then something happened which I have been trying to tell these forty-five years, but it grows on me so that the job has become an elephant.

(d) He baptized me with the Holy Ghost and fire, burning up the college president (as my conference had made me), and the Free Mason, and the Odd Fellow, as I was chaplain in both lodges; burning up the water-god and all my idols, in a bonfire in which sectarianism, politics, lodgery and worldliness in all its forms and phases went down in an ashpile. I had wandered in the wilderness the nineteen years, often climbing Pisgah's Mount and with

longing eyes viewing the promised land. I could
tarry no longer, not even to perform the funeral
rites of my old friends. Dashing away at race horse
speed, I walked out on the swelling Jordan, the sum-
mary of all my doubts and fears, and the enginery
of my fond ambitions; thus heroically as if his swelling had been a marble pavement. An unseen hand
splits his impetuous volume in twain, permitting me
to pass over dry shod. I shouted down the walls of
Jericho and marched as Joshua's army for the grand
interior; stand on the battle mount of Bethhoron;
see the sun halt over Gibeon and the moon over the
valley of Aigolon, till Joshua has time to finish his
battle and thirty one kings lose their heads and all
South Canaan capitulates. Then in Joshua's army I
marched to the great north; stand by the waters of
Merom, confronted by the combined kingdoms of the
north under the leadership of Jabin, king of Hazor,
till we see them all go down in flood. I peregrinate
the land, singing jubilantly, "I've reached the land
of corn and wine," etc.

(e) I shall always believe that if I had let the
water god alone and in the dim light which shown
around me in the absence of all sanctified testimonies,
I would have prayed through and received the victory
in less than half those memorable nineteen years, I
spent in the howling wilderness. Two great arguments against immersion: one it is not so much as
mentioned in all the Bible. There are two words,
katapontidzo (Matt. 18: 6), and **buthidzo**, (1 Tim.
5: 9), both of which mean to immerse, i. e., to sink
and never come up, which is the meaning of immersion. If you get subject out you have to use another word immersion; whereas immersion puts it
down and never does take it out. But neither of
these Greek words are ever used a single time to
define **baptidzo.** My amanuensis asks, "Where do

we get immersion if it is not in the Bible?" We
answer, from the heathen, who practice it all the
time now, as I have traveled all around the world
and have seen with my own eyes. The heathen are
more religious than we are, so anxious to be saved
that they wear themselves out with the religion as
they have no knowledge of the Savior, who alone can
take away sin and give you rest in His arms. They
toil indefatigably, serving their gods, persuant to
the direction of their priests, and never get rid of
sin.

(f) India, with her three hundred millions of
people and a great host of learned Brahman priests,
is the most religious country in the world, probably
owing to the fact that the priests are so many and
they are very industrious and aggressive, devoting
their whole time to preaching and teaching the
people; as the castification of the whole population
into the four grades, the Brahmans, first caste; sol-
diers, second; merchants and mechanics, third, and
the uneducated laborers, including the great rank
and file of the population, the fourth caste, besides
many very poor people, who do not live in houses,
but without like animals and have no caste. As
these castes are not allowed to transcend, the privileges of their order; thus putting an awful yoke
of bondage on the people, so tight and heavy that
God's own hand alone can break it. This state of
things leaves the Brahman priests nothing to do
but preach and teach the people. They teach them
that the waters of the great and beautiful Ganges
and Jumna are holy and competent to wash sins
away. As the low castes are so poor, they cannot
travel a great distance to these holy rivers, the
priests have them construct tanks in all parts of the
country remote from these rivers and supply them
with water from the nearest river. Then they con-

secrate them and tell the people that the waters are
just as holy, by virtue of their consecration as the
Ganges and Jumna.

While preaching in Madras, the largest city in
South India, a million people, I gave especial attention to the holy tank occupying a whole square of
the city; elegantly constructed with nice stone floor
and beautiful hewn stone steps descending from each
of the four streets on all sides, so thousands of people
could descend simultaneously and wash their sins
away. On the east side is the great Pantheon in
which all the gods of India, 330,000,000 are wor-
shipped. In travelling throughout that great country, six thousand miles, I saw them immersing everywhere to wash their sins away. The Brahman priests
preach precisely the doctrine of the Campbellites
and Mormons in this country, immersion for remis-
sion of sins; but unlike the latter who will only immerse you one time in life, they say, go in every
time you sin. As they have no Savior to take the
sin personality out of them and give them the victory, and their consciences are very tender, so they
think that if they accidentally step on a bug or
worm and kill it, they are guilty of murder and consequently will have to go again and have their sins
washed away. The fact that immersion is not once
mentioned in all the Bible, nor any other word which
has that meaning ever used for baptism, proves de-
monstratively its pagan origin, so abundantly corroborated by its universal practice among them.
Therefore when under the Emperor Constantine who
was converted to Christianity A. D. 321, and became
exceedingly zealous and did his best to get all the
people in the world to give up their idols and turn
Christians.

(g) The preceding is corroborated by the fact
that immersion was never heard of in the Church

till after every Apostle had gone to heaven, and the heathen brought it in.   Lactantious, the oldest historian in the Christian era, who lived and wrote in the third century when the matter was rife in popular memory; people still living who had seen the Apostles and been baptized by them, and especially their children on all sides; testifies: "John the Baptist sprinkled, Peter sprinkled and Christ sent His Apostles that they should sprinkle the nations.   This is the testimony of the Apostolic Age.   "Brother Godbey, I thought the historians certified to immersion."   I know they do, Neander, Wilson, Orchard and Mocheim, but when did they live?   All of them in the eighteenth and nineteenth centuries, i. e., in our time and none of them quote any ancient authority.   Consequently it was simply their opinion, which is worth no more than yours or mine.   An ancient matter must be certified by an ancient witness.   The witnesses quoted by immersionists all lived fifteen hundred years to late to know anything about it. while not one of them quote an ancient author. Therefore it is nonsense to tinker with them.

Chapter II.

TESTIMONY OF JOHN THE BAPTIST, JESUS, PETER, PAUL, MARK, LUKE AND APOLLOS

Mark 1: 8, which includes Peter as he dictated it while Mark wrote it; Luke 3: 16, which includes the testimony of Paul who dictated it; Acts 1: 5, which is the personal testimony of Jesus who spoke it, also including Paul the author and Luke the amanuensis; Acts 11: 16, which includes the testimony of Paul and Luke, and Hebrews 10: 22, which is the testimony of Apollos the author, (not Paul as you think. In the chapter immediately preceding Hebrews, Paul certifies that his authorship is in all his epistles. It is not in Hebrews showing positively that Paul never wrote it. It was without a name till six hundred years ago when the pope ordered them to put Paul's name in it. Of course he did not know. I know he never wrote it because he under the inspiration of the Holy Ghost thus certifies. Besides it is not Pauline style, which is very plain while this epistle is quite eloquent. It has no name, but I agree with the leading critics, Dean Alford and others who give it to Apollos, the eloquent Apostle.) In these five scriptures, containing this brilliant band of inspired witnesses; they all certify that John and the apostles handle the water and not the people. How do I know this? Because the Greek word **hudati** in every one of these is in the dative of instrumentality without a preposition; whereas if they had immersed them, it would have been **eis to hudor.** As I have passed my eightieth year and am looking on the last mile post on my heaven-bound journey and electrified by the angelic songs beyond the last river, I shall soon in His super-abounding mercy, lay the armor down, on the gory field and fly away to the Mount of Victory.

Pardon me for inserting a word from the funeral dirge of Sir John Moore; slowly and sadly we laid him down from the field of his fame, fresh and gory; we curve not a line nor raised not a stone, but left him alone in his glory. No useless coffin inclosed his breast, nor in sheet nor shroud we bound him; but he lay like a warrior taking his rest with his martial cloak around him. I have requested my family to spend none of the Lord's money uselessly in my interment, nor give me any tombstone, as I am more than willing to risk the resurrecting angels. Soon I shall meet this apostolic band on the heavenly highlands, who will thank me for correcting the popular mistake, which has hung like a nightmare on the Church since the Dark Ages; admitted the heathen with their ordinances and ceremonies and fastened this yoke on coming generations, superinducing the useless labor and exposure, unto premature death in countless instances, requiring the preacher to take the candidate in his arms and wade into the cold, flooded river, stand there, put him down and lift him up and walk out, thus administering a burdensome ceremony, perilous to the health of both subject and administrator, and utterly unheard of in the Bible which mentions no baptism but the little harmless, though beautifully significant sprinkle. (Ezek. 36: 25; Isa. 2: 15; Heb. 9: 19; 1 Cor. 10 ch.; Psa. 77.) This word **hudati** in the five citations beginning this chapter, giving the testimony of Jesus, John the Baptist, Peter, Paul, Mark, Luke and Apollos, is not preceded by any preposition. Hence there is no dodging the conclusion and swinging off on prepositions, as the Word settles the conclusion that they handled the water and not the people. This is corroborated by all the statuary. I saw in the catacombs of Rome, which were made in the first centuries of the Christian era, Jesus standing and John pouring the water on His head; making Him a personal specialty in view of His pre-eminence; whereas the multitudes He served with the hyssop, dipping it in the water and swinging it over them, as you see this day the Catholic priest sprinkled his congregation with the holy water.

(h) When we entered the house of Judas in Damascus where Saul of Tarsus was converted under the ministry of Ananias, our whole band of eight Holiness preachers broke out in a shout at the sight of Paul an Ananias in life size statuary, exhibiting his baptism, Ananias pouring the water on his head. That house is this day a Greek Christian Church. We hear and see much immersion in this country, where we know nothing, aboriginally. When we go to the old world, where the patriarchs, prophets, Jesus and His apostles all spent their lives and whence their knowledge all comes, we never find a trace nor track of immersion, but all testimony, statuary, historical and traditionary, is in harmony with the Bible record. The ordinance is not the thing at all; but simply the sign of it. There is but one baptism (Eph. 4: 5) that Jesus gives with the Holy Ghost and fire, in every case by effusion. It is simply a shame to hear the pitiful and pusilanimous tergiversations, which the immersionists poke off on the people in order to blind their eyes to the plain beautiful, unmistakable truth of the Bible; even saying that the baptism of the Holy Ghost is immersion, in flat contradiction of Jesus and His apostles and prophets, certifying in both Testaments that the Spirit is poured and falls on the people, as the fiery symbol fell on them at Pentecost.

(i) These perversions of God's plain Word, dem-

onstrate to all honest, intelligent people the falsity
of the cause they are rallied to support; as the truth
never needs anything of that kind. God says it so
plain that "way-faring men though fools shall not
err therein." (Isaiah 35th chapter.) Their grand
citadel, the "burial," is simply hell-hatched humbuggery, as they apply it to the physical body, in
flat contradiction to the plain Word, that it is the
"old man," i. e., devil nature, hereditary in every
human heart. This perversion of God's plain Word,
substituting the mortal body for the body of
sin, could only eminate from the bottomless pit,
the chicanery of Satan, to keep you from getting the
sin principle destroyed, which actually means your
damnation.

(j) They capped the climax by boldly certifying
that no one has ever been baptized with the Holy
Ghost since the apostles on the day of Pentecost, al-
leging the inseparability of the miracles which they
performed, (which were really extraordinary, to ex-
pedite the launching of the Gospel Church) from the
Savior's baptism, which is indispensible to the salvation of every soul. In this, they take the bit in
their teeth and assume the right to interpret His
Word, conservatively to their own idolatrous dog-
matism in the maintenance of immersion, as the
sine qua non of salvation instead of Jesus; thus making it a god and actually promoting it above the
work of Christ, as they make it the ultimatum in
every case, and no such a thing as personal salvation
until it is received, climaxing everything else in
their bogus curriculum, which they lay down for
the people to observe in order to be saved as you
see it winds up with the water god, giving him the
pre-eminence over Jesus.

Chapter III.

THE PREPOSITIONAL ARGUMENT

Aside from the gross and unscriptural perversion of Romans 6th and Col. 2nd chapter, relative to the burial which they apply to the mortal body, they run off on the poor, ignorant people that awful hell-hatched humbuggery, construing the mortal body, the body of sin and a flat contradiction of Paul. (2 Cor. 6-18.) Every sin is without the body, i. e. entirely outside of it, illustrated by the fornicator who sins against his own body, also the drunkard, little by little destroying their bodies by sin; forcing the poor body to suffer a thousand deaths and go down to a premature grave, tumbling into an awful hell.

(k) Thus the Bible plainly reveals that this tenement in which we live is not the sinner; God gave it to us to use for His glory and He proposes to come and live with us in it Himself. So the Bible nowhere intimates that the mortal body is a sinner, but says, "The soul that sinneth it shall die." Therefore the body of sin is a spirituality and not a materiality. It is hereditary in every human soul, devil nature, depravity transmitted from the fallen Adam and will prove Satan's millstone around our necks and drag us down to hell, and as hell has no bottom, he will continue to pull us into a deeper abyss of quenchless damnation, through the flight of endless ages. Therefore if you do not get this sin personality destroyed you are ruined forever. No human device can do it. Adam the Second alone can slay Adam the first. Now in case of the Campbellites, they put the preacher in place of Jesus, the water in place of the Holy Spirit and your poor mortal body in place of the body of sin, the devil nature, hereditary in the heart, and the result is that they literally humbug you out of your soul. So like Dives, you will die looking out for heaven, but find hell. The poor Campbellite preacher, Mormon prophet or Catholic priest can never do anything for you when the devil comes. The angels came for Lazarus and carried him with shouts to Abraham's bosom—the Old Testament paradise; meanwhile the myrmidons from the bottomless pit came for Dives and took him, despite the robed priests and church officials and wealthy members, who wept around him, feeling sure that he was going to heaven and he went down to hell.

(l) This awful infidelity, making the mortal body the body of sin, and putting it in the water instead of nailing the sin personality to the cross till it is dead, substituting the preacher and churchisms and manipulations of the Conqueror of Mt. Calvary, who alone is able to take the devil at the throat to deliver the person from his stygian grip, impoverish Satan, bankrupt hell, and bring the world to Christ in adoring homage at His feet. Besides the burial argument, which they so defiantly and atrociously pervert, running their hell-hatched humbuggery on the people by wholesale, leading the unspiritual captive **ad libitum**; they have no other argument except the prepositional, which is the weakest of all arguments and never should be used in any case involving life and salvation, from the simple fact that the preposition is no essential part of any language; like the conjunction, it is only connectional. Consequently when I send a telegram I never use it, because they charge me with every word and the preposition is an unessential.

The reason why we have the statement "into the water" and "out" is because King James' trans-

lators, who did their work more than three hundred
years ago, when we were still under the shadow of
the Dark Ages, so little light and learning in the
world, for them or anybody else, and they had all
been immersed three times, which was the current
practice of the Dark Ages, that dismal night of
time; meanwhile not one man in a thousand nor one
woman in twenty thousand could read or write, and
sacerdotalism had the Church in its dismal grip—
sin, ignorance and superstition, Satan trinity, in the
succession of the beautiful angels: faith hope and
love—God's trinity driven away by the dark iniqui-
ties which flooded the Church, indissolubly wedded
to the world. It was customary to take the people in
a state of utter nudity; the men and the women in
separate rooms; the latter served by the deaconesses
and dipped the body right side downward in the
name of the Father, lifted up, turn it around and
dip it left side downward in the name of the Son,
then lifting up, turned with the face foremost then
dipped in the name of the Holy Ghost. In this way
the translators of our Bible had received baptism.
That was antecedently to the glorious light which
has risen upon the whole world in the last three
centuries; when the translators themselves believed
that trine-immersion was the Apostolic practice.
Recently Dr. Dowie made a great stir in this country
attempting to restore the trine-immersion; but signally failed. He verily believed that went back to
the Apostolic Age—a serious mistake, as no one can
trace it beyond the third century, when the heathen
millions pouring in brought the immersion, which
they afterward magnified into trine-immersion; ev-
entually a state of nudity, with other ceremonies.
not now practiced anywhere. The reason why we
have in King James the statement, "Into the water"
and "out," is because they had received it in that

way and the long practice through the rolling centuries of time's midnight, while there was so little knowledge in the world, had fastened it till they believed that it was the primitive practice. Therefore it supervened in the translation of the normal effect of water on the brain, which is so prevalent now; known in the medical world hydrocephalus and by the old world pronounced incurable. Yet rest assured Jesus can cure it, as I had it badly when I constrained that Methodist preacher to immerse me, in order to give me the victory for which my heart did cry and sigh, but only finding the clouds darker and the fogs denser and the inward enemy the more incorrigible as all my efforts to drown old Adam proved a failure and inpedimental to the inward purity and Messianic coronation in my heart and life for which my soul did sigh and my spirit cry. When Jesus gave me the wonderful fiery baptism forty-five years ago, burning up lodgery, sectarianism, politics and worldliness, in its diversified forms and phases, He effectually burned up my hydrocephalus. Therefore I recommend Him for all. This is our victory, yea even our faith. (1 John 5: 4.)

(m) All those statements "into the water" and "out of the water" were put in by King James' translators, because they had water on the brain. Philip and the Eunuch (Acts 8 ch.) is about the strongest—they both went down into the water and both came up out of the water. I have eight times visited that place, celebrated with guides and guide books and well known to all. It is on the road from Jerusalem to Gaza, due south about eighteen miles from the former; the road running between the Great Sea on the west forty miles and the Dead Sea on the east thirty miles, each way down the mountain; the distance to short for a river as the water does not sufficiently accumulate—no river nearer than the Jordan, seventy miles. It is simply a water spout on the left side of the road, and every time I recognized it long before arrival by the group of women standing around, each holding a waterpot— an earthen vessel, jug shape, different sizes—each waiting her turn to put the mouth of her jug under the spout and hold it till it runs full; the water a valuable quality much appreciated and carried to a great distance; all caught in its fall so no stream is there to run away. You remember when Jesus was preaching in Capernaum they called on Him and Peter to pay their temple assessment, thirty cents per capita for the support of the temple, assessed on every Jew; and they did not have the money. He told Peter to go down to the sea, toss in a hook, catch the first fish that bites, examine its mouth and find a stater, a coin of sixty cents. Peter went, caught the fish, returned and paid their temple assessments. Do you believe Peter waded in waist deep to catch that fish with hook and line? You know he did not as none but an idiot would have done it and Peter was one of the most intelligent men who ever lived on the earth.

"Bro. Godbey, why do you ask this question?" Because the very same verb, **porino** and preposition, **eis** are used in both cases, therefore if you do not believe that Peter waded in waist deep to catch the fish, you need not think that Philip and the Eunuch waded into the water for the baptism.

When I visited that place on my second tour, 1899, I was accompanied by my son-in-law, Brother Hill and Brother Paine of California. When the carriage arrived opposite the spring and halted for us to see the sight, I kept my seat as I had been there twice and satisfied my curiosity; two young men leaping cut ran to it, caught the water and drank and brought me a drink. Those women were all barefoot and standing in a puddle of waste water, which had fallen from the spout while exchanging vessels and the ground very hard, retained it. Therefore I saw them both go down into the water and both of them came up out of it, just as it says of Philip and the Eunuch. When they got in the carriage, I asked them if they got their feet wet and they said, "No." Though they went into the water and came out again there was not enough there to get into their shoes. Hence you see that the statement does not prove anything in the way of immersion. This was called the Fountain of Beth-Horem, as recorded by Eusebius, the historian of the fifth century, the noble preacher of the Gospel, until Philip baptized the eunuch there, when in commemoration of that historic event they changed the name and they have ever since called it Philip's Fountain. Bedaker's Guide-book is the standard of all that country. He lived there thirty years, traveled everywhere and wrote the book and certifies in it that this is really the place where Philip baptized the eunuch. As to the statement, "went down to the water," the down simply means out of the chariot, as **katabaino,** went down, is antithetical to **alabaino** a few verses above when the enunch invited him to come up into the chariot with him and read him the Word of the Lord which he was then reading in the 53rd chapter of Isaiah. He was reading from the Septuagint, i. e., the Greek version of the Old Testament, which had no division into chapters. Look at it and you see that he had just read the last verse of the 52nd chapter, which says, in reference to Christ, "So shall He sprinkle many nations," i. e., send the Gospel throughout the whole world, preaching, making disciples and baptizing the same as the commission, (Matt. 28: 19) : "Go disciple all nations,

baptizing them." Every other case in the New Testament where it speaks of going in and coming out,
is like this; perfectly correctly translated, going
to and coming from and no evidence of any entrance.
The people generally think that it says Jesus went
down into the water and came up out of it which is
not true for it does not say that He went down into
it, but it does say that He came up straightway out
of the water but is well known to be a wrong translation as the Greek word **apo** in that passage, never
does mean "out of," but simply away from. When
John baptized Him, as that was His inauguration into
His official Messiahship, He immediately went away
into the wilderness to be tempted of Satan. Luke
says when He was baptized, that while He was pray-
ing, the Holy Spirit in the form of a dove descended
on Him.

(n) It is a fact attested by all translators that
the Jordan, at the place where Israel crossed and
John preached and baptized is fifteen feet deep at
low water and as it is in the rapids only ten miles
above its effuse into the Dead Sea, the current moves
with velocity of a mountain torrent and no man can
stand in it. Thus in the providence of God the
bold old Jordan bears his own testimony to the truth
certified by John the Baptist, Jesus, Paul, Peter,
Mark, Luke and Apollos, that they handled the
water and not the people; as in the five strong,
passages given previously we have **hudati** with water,
the dative of instrumentality, just as I walk with
a cane and my amanuensis writes with a pencil. So
there is no mistake about it, they manipulated the
water and not the people.

(o) When the Texas boys, John and Edward
Roberts and Allie Irick, traveled with me round the
world; pursuant to their request I immersed them in
the Jordan, which in the many difficulties we en-

countered perfected my conviction against the conclusion that such a thing was ever known in the
Bible times. When we had decended from the Wilderness of Judea down into the Jordan plain, the young
men spoke to my old guide, Sukrey Hishuch, in the
carriage with us, who was born in Jerusalem and has
spent his whole life there; educated for the work of
dragoman, which he has pursued all his life, con-
stantly traveling over that entire country, escorting
pilgrims from all parts of Christendom. When they
broke the news to him he flared up, much excited and
said he would not permit it as he had seen men
drowned there, so he would tolerate nothing of the
kind. The young men proceeded to plead with him,
observing that they had come a long way at their
own expense and they thought he ought to permit
them to enjoy all the privileges. Then when he
found them persistent, he gave way to deep grief;
tears gushing copiously from his eyes and deluging
his brown face, and the young men recognized from
maneuvers, that he was alarmed over his financial
responsibility as a dragoman, like a Railroad Co. is
responsible under law for the people committed to his
charge. He feared that some of us would get drowned and our families would sue him and break him up
financially. The young men proceeded to relieve him
of all financial responsibility as they could swim
like ducks and were not afraid of any waters, consequently he gave them no more attention, but as I
didn't relieve him of responsibility, he focalized his
attention on me. On arrival I hunted in vain for a
good place to go down, as the bank was a sudden
offset and the river fifteen feet deep and flowing
like a mountain torrent. I walked along and hunted
for a good place to go down, but signally failing,
having reached a little indentation where the earth
had broken and fallen, concluded I would go in there.

Having gone through the preliminary ceremonies
I proceeded to go down; my guide, a big stout man,
and the armed escort, also stalwart, going along and
holding me tight so if I slipped they could lift me
out as the water is always so muddy you cannot see
an inch below its surface, and if a person should
suddenly go under he would be utterly out of sight
and lost. Held by those two strong men I walked
down with my staff, searching in vain for a good
place to locate my feet.

(p)   Having reached sufficient depth to handle
them, looking back to see them following me, for I
did not undertake to lead them in, failing to see them
I looked in front and behold they are all out on the
swelling Jordan swimming. I beckoned to John, the
nearest one and he swims to me. Then I say the
ceremony and put him under and let him go as I
could not have led him out. Then I beckon to Allie,
who swims to me and I serve him and let him go to
swim out **ad libitum;** finally Edward swims to me and
I immerse him and let him go to swim out. Then
my guide and armed escort led me out. N. B. I was
not in the current, which was fifteen feet deep and
would have been impossible, besides it was so swift
I could not have stood in it; I was only in an eddy
at the bank. The bold old Jordan tells his own story
and forever refutes the foolish idea that John stood
in his rolling, merky flood and handled all these people; an utter impossibility.

(q)   I have often heard preachers say that Jesus
was immersed and He is our example: an utter mistake all the way through, neither He or any one else
did John immerse, because he said that he did with
water what Jesus was going to do with the Holy
Ghost and fire, which he poured on them, so the
Spirit and the fire fell on them. If he had not done
with water the very same thing he would have used

a different word, whereas he used the very same to reveal what he did with the water and Jesus would do with the Holy Ghost and fire. You may give directions to two persons to perform different actions, as you will find that you are obliged to use different words to administer the order. If you say the same word, both parties will go and do the same thing. "Does not the Greek **baptidzo** always mean immerse?" It never does in the New Testament. I have before me the highest authorities in the world, Dr. Jno. Schluesner of Germany, who has expounded the Greek Testament into volumes the size of the margin Bible, giving every word in it in extenso; thus exhaustively explaining every word. On **baptidzo** he gives to immerse as a primary definition, applied to ships sinking, but it never means immerse, i. e., to come up and even in that definition it does not signify the ministration of immersion baptism, because they not only put you down but raise you up. This means to go down and never come up. Having given that primary definition, thus he moves on: **sed in hac significatione numquam in novo testamento**—never used in the New Testament, but in this signification it is never used in the New Testament. Then he goes on to specify how it is used in the sense of effusion and gives every case in the New Testament and finds no immersion. This lexicon stands at the very top of the world's authority and the definition all given in Latin because the scholars of all nations read Latin and consequently they can use the book in every country under heaven. Robinson's dictionary stands at the front of this continent and gives the definition in English and persues the same course, we see Schluesner in Latin. He goes on to allude to the baptistaries still to be seen, having been made and used in the Apostolic Age and all too small, thus demonstrating the fact it was not the

primitive practice of the Church. I hold in my hand
the critical Greek Testament by Hort, Wescott, the
recognized standard of the world, the consensues of
all the critics. It has a lexicon explaining all the
words in the New Testament and does not give
immerse as a definition of baptism at all, but simply
gives to cleanse, to wash, to administer baptism, thus
in harmony with our Savior's own preaching throughout in which He only defines it by **catharidzo,** which
has no meaning but to purify.

(r)   And every other place in the New Testament coincides with this, simply meaning to purify;
thus showing up the transcendent importance of his
own baptism, which every human soul must have or
be forever lost, as he came to destroy the works of
the devil, which is sin. (1 John 3: 8).   Therefore
he alone is competent to this work, which He per-
forms when he baptizes us.   Consequently Campbellism gives no one a chance for his soul, because it
denies the baptism of the Holy Ghost to any one
except the apostles, in the face of the plain Word.
(Acts 2: 38, 39) : "The promise is to you and to
your children and to all who are afar off, even so
many as the Lord our God shall call." "What promise?"   Why, the baptism of the Holy Ghost, which
was the great interest of that occasion, not restricted
to the apostles, but for all whom the Lord would
ever call through His ministry and Spirit—all the
world.   The **ipse dixit** of Campbellism, restricting
the baptism of the Holy Ghost to the people who had
received power to work miracles by the Holy Ghost,
is contradictory of our Savior's definition, running
throughout the whole Bible, which is simply a purification, and that means the removal of all the pollu-
tion Satan ever put in you; simply giving you a
clean heart.   The great work of Christ is appropri-
ately expressed in the word cathriasm, now English,

though a transformation of the Greek **cathargo,** and means the entire purifying work of the Holy Spirit in the human heart; eliminating everything Satan put there.

(q) Regeneration is sanctification; thus in personality conquered and grace given to keep down till utterly destroyed by the baptism of the Holy Ghost and fire, purifying the heart from the last and least residum of the carnal mind and perfecting Holiness in the fear of God. All the enumerable ceremonials of the Levitical law in which they had so many baptisms, (quite a diversity, Heb. 9: 10, diverse baptisms), in so many ways are liable to contract ceremonial defilement, which disqualified for tabernacle service or the privileges of the temple and the Holy Campus, and even the synagogue until the water of purification was sprinkled on them by a ceremonially clean person. While water baptism takes in all these catharisms, all administered by sprinkling, (Ezek. 36: 25), "I will sprinkle clean water on you and from all your filthiness and idols I will cleanse you, and a new heart will I give unto you and a new spirit will I put within you." Thus conversion is mentioned twice in the commission given by Ezekiel 600 years before Matthew. "And take away your stony heart and give you a heart of flesh," and sanctification told twice over and no one able to see it all beautifully signify "I will sprinkle clean water on you," i. e., the ordinance of baptism everywhere concomitant with the preaching of the Gospel.

(s) Origin, the greatest scholar and author of the Apostolic Age—his father and grandfather both preachers of the Gospel, both suffered martyrdom: his father when the boy was only seventeen years old; who, at his father's martyrdom, took up the silver trumpet he laid down for the golden harp and began to blow it, running for his life from one coun-

try to another, so evading his persecutors as to live
to be seventy years old; but finally his enemies over-
take him; he sealed his faith with his blood and went
up to join his father and grandfather with a mar-
tyr's crown also glittering on his brow. In the providence of God he was the most voluminous writer
in the Church, author of sixty books; among them
commentaries on the Bible, having the honor to be
the first man who ever wrote commentaries on the
Bible. In his exegesis of 1 Kings, writing up the
transaction on Mt. Carmel, describing Elijah pouring
the water on the altar, he uses the word **baptidzo;**
thus writing it up as a baptism. **Baptidzo** is a pure
Greek word and Origin was a native Greek, a mem-
ber of a family of Greek philosophers, enjoined the
highest culture of the world as Greece stood at the
top of the learned world. Therefore in his commentaries you have a grand and irrefutable definition
of **baptidzo,** showing that it is fully satisfied when
defined as an effusion. The awful sophistry of people wedded to a creed, leads them to every conceiv-
able perversion and transgression. Surely no one
could make an immersion out of that . It would take
Noah's flood to do it, because it occured on the summit of Mt. Carmel, great and high.

(t)   The Latin Bible was made in the Apostolic
Age and is understood to have Apostolic endorse-
ment. Immerse is a pure Latin word, while baptize
is a pure Greek word; both of them being adopted
into the English language. If immerse was the meaning of baptize we would surely find it in the Latin
Bible currently used to define **baptidzo.** It is an in-
disputable fact that it does not occur anywhere in
the Latin Bible, which is demonstrative proof that
it is not a definition of the word. They contend that
tingo, which does occur in the Latin Bible means
immerse, which is interiable. Look in Webster's dic-

tionary for ting and you will find it is a solism of the Latin **tingo.**

When I was studying the Latin language, reading Horace, the celebrated poet, he gave the case of an old Roman, so very rich that he sprinkled the pavement around his house with wine, in order that they might emit a delicious fragrance in the circunambient atmosphere. You know that there was no chance to immerse the pavement into the wine, but the wine was sprinkled on it. The great revival at Pentecost, when 3,000 were converted to the Christhood of Jesus during the morning service and 5,000 in the afternoon giving the paradoxical agrate of 8,000 during the day, converted and added to the Gospel Church. These were all baptized as it says. Jerusalem is a mountain city, built high upon Mt. Zion, too high to dig wells, as in case you would dig you would get no water. At the very time it was supplied with water from Solomon's pools, a dozen miles away in the mountains and brought hither by an aqueduct. I have been in Jerusalem early in June at the time of the Pentecost. If I got a drink of water I had to buy it. I never bought it. I never bought any, but always bought the lemonade, the best in the world and the cheapest I ever knew. The impression frequently entertained that these people were sinners converted to God is untrue, as it says. that there were at Jerusalem, devout people from every nation under heaven. The Jews in the Babylonian captivity had been dispersed to the ends of the earth as that empire was universal and had come from all lands to attend their great annual campmeeting; thus refuting the prevalent idea that the ten tribes were lost; they were on hand and their representatives sent in from all parts of the world. As a rule the most godly people are selected to go to great assemblies as representatives of God's king-

dom. This wonderful ten days' prayer-meeting had
reached the closing Sabbath when the Lord baptized
them with the Holy Ghost and fire, so gloriously
sanctifying the 120 that they swept down like a
thundering avalanche from the Alpine summit;
shouting so loudly as to magnitize this multitude
over on Mt. Moriah, the Holy Campus, the last day
of the feast. The shouts were so uproarous and
aroused their curiosity, that they come running a
mile across the Tyrubian Valley and ascend Mt. Zion
thrilled with curiosity to know what it meant. Peter
the Seer, so wrapped in heavenly flame, leads off
in a sermon, which was an actual thunder clap from
beginning to end, showing them by the prophecies
that this man they had crucified fifty days ante-
cendently was none other than the Shiloh of proph-
ecy, the Christ of God, the coming Messiah, the Redeemer of Israel and the Savior of the world.

(u)   These godly Jews had been waiting four
thousand years the coming of the world's redeemer,
since the days of Abel on the constant outlook. The
thunderbolts and lightning crash sermon of Peter
pouring on them in torrents of fire, their own prophecies of the coming Christ, so wonderfully fulfilled,
that the people on all sides see the irresistable fact
and scream aloud, "What shall we do to be saved!"
He responds, "Repent and let each one of you be
baptized, (i. e., each one who has repented be baptized) in the name of Jesus Christ, unto the remis-
sion of your sins and ye shall receive the gift of the
Holy Ghost," i. e., this wonderful baptism of the
Holy Ghost which he had already given to the disciples. There is an obivious error in King James,
which makes repentance and baptize as ordinant
commandments. Repent is second person, plural
number and applied to all of them, followed by the
clause, "Let each one of you be baptized," in the

third person, singular, each being distributive pronouns, referring to antecedent which is subject of repent, mean, "Let each one of you who has repented be baptized in the name of the Lord." When man repents God always forgives. Therefore the baptism was only to those who repented. Next verse is wonderfully explicit and consolitory; for "the promise is unto you and unto your children, unto all who are afar off, even so many as the Lord our God shall call." That is the promise of the baptism of the Holy Ghost, which was the transcendent interest of that occasion, so persistently and emphatically prophesied by John the Baptist and constituted the crowning glory of our Savior's ministry, for which His vicarious atonement was the great and indespensible antecedent, while the baptism of the Holy Ghost and fire, which was to follow, consummates the grand restitution of the human soul, for which He was made manifest. (1 John 3: 8.) This baptism which Jesus gives with the Holy Ghost and fire is the great **sine qua non,** without which the Lord has decreed that no one shall see Him. (Heb. 12: 14.) **Baptidzo,** baptize, is perfectly synonymous with **hagiadzo,** sanctify, because Jesus defines both by the very same word, **catharidzo,** which has no meaning but to purify, literally, take the world out of you, as it is from **ga,** the earth, and **alpha,** not. Therefore both of the words simply mean to take out of you what Satan put in you, i. e., depravity, devil nature.

(v) The great trouble with immersion is its magnitude, so much of it, putting the body in water all over, that you are constrained to recognize it, not only at the time but the normal trend is through your whole life and consequently lose sight of the one essential baptism which Jesus gives with the Holy Ghost.

How strange people can be so eggregiously humbugged by false teachers with the plain Word of the Lord conspicuously before their eyes. Be sure you get Jesus to baptize you and beware of the water god and concomitant delusions. Meet me in heaven.

W. B. GODBEY.

www.ingramcontent.com/pod-product-compliance
Lightning Source LLC
Chambersburg PA
CBHW030313030426
42337CB00012B/692